# Skills Builders

SARAH

**YEAR 4**

# SPELLING AND VOCABULARY

## Nicola Morris

# Acknowledgements

Every effort has been made to trace all copyright holders, but if any have been inadvertently overlooked, the Publishers will be pleased to make the necessary arrangements at the first opportunity.

Although every effort has been made to ensure that website addresses are correct at time of going to press, Rising Stars cannot be held responsible for the content of any website mentioned in this book. It is sometimes possible to find a relocated web page by typing in the address of the home page for a website in the URL window of your browser.

Hachette UK's policy is to use papers that are natural, renewable and recyclable products and made from wood grown in sustainable forests. The logging and manufacturing processes are expected to conform to the environmental regulations of the country of origin.

ISBN: 978-1-78339-721-1

Text, design and layout © 2016 Rising Stars UK Ltd

First published in 2016 by Rising Stars UK Ltd
Rising Stars UK Ltd, An Hachette UK Company
Carmelite House 50 Victoria Embankment
London EC4Y 0DZ

www.risingstars–uk.com

All facts are correct at time of going to press.

Author: Nicola Morris
Educational Consultant: Madeleine Barnes
Publisher: Laura White
Illustrator: Emily Skinner
Logo design: Amparo Barrera, Kneath Associates Ltd
Design: Julie Martin
Typesetting: Newgen
Cover design: Amparo Barrera, Kneath Associates Ltd
Project Manager: Seonaid Loader, Out of House Publishing
Copy Editor: Claire Pearce-Jones
Proofreader: Jennie Clifford
Software development: Alex Morris

British Library Cataloguing–in–Publication Data
A CIP record for this book is available from the British Library.
Printed by Liberduplex S.L., Barcelona, Spain

# Contents

## SPELLING

## VOCABULARY

All of the answers can be found online. To get access, simply register or login at **www.risingstars-uk.com**.

# 1 Word classes

We need to know what the word classes are so that we can talk about how words are related and how they can be changed from one class to another. There are different types of word classes.

- A **noun** is the name of a thing or idea.
  **school, Manchester, freedom**

- An **adjective** is a describing word.
  **strict, golden, delightful**

- A **verb** is a doing or being word.
  **running, am, was**

- An **adverb** describes a verb.
  **soon, angrily, quickly**

- A **preposition** gives more information about a noun.
  **on, above, beside**

## Activity 1

Draw a table in your book and sort these words into the correct word classes.

~~football~~   ~~sunny~~   ~~India~~   ~~shout~~   ~~clock~~

~~cooked~~   ~~hopeful~~   ~~gentle~~   ~~share~~

~~air~~   ~~crowd~~   ~~want~~   ~~famous~~

| Nouns | Adjectives | Verbs |
|-------|------------|-------|
| india<br>Clock<br>air | Sunny<br>hopeful<br>gentle<br>famous | Shout<br>football<br>Cooked<br>Share<br>Crowd<br>Want |

## Activity 2

Write down the word class for the word <u>underlined</u> in each sentence.

**a)** It was a <u>delicious</u> cake. _delicious_

**b)** The aeroplane <u>flew</u> overhead. _flew_

**c)** Matilda chose a new <u>coat</u> for winter. _coat_

**d)** The children played <u>noisily</u> in the playground. _noisily_

**e)** The stream flowed <u>under</u> the bridge. _under_

## Activity 3

Complete each of these sentences, using a word of your choice from the missing word class.

**a)** The _girl_ ran down the street. (noun)

**b)** Kian rode on his _new_ bicycle. (adjective)

**c)** The children _walked_ in the classroom. (verb)

**d)** The dragon swooped down _quickly_. (adverb)

**e)** She hid _behind_ the tree. (preposition)

## Activity 4

**a)** Which words give us more information about the **noun** 'dog'?

They were looking for a dog with a <u>blue collar</u> around its neck.

**b)** Which word gives more information about the **verb** 'writing'?

Zaynab was writing <u>neatly</u>.

## Investigate!

What is happening around you?

**a)** Write down the **verbs** that explain what people are doing.

**b)** Write down the **adverbs** to explain how they are doing it.

**c)** Write down the **prepositions** to explain where they are doing it.

# 2 Apostrophes for contraction

A **contraction** is the shortened form of a word. The **apostrophe** shows where a letter or letters would be if the words were written in full.

wasn't ——→ was not
we've ——→ we have

## Activity 1

Which **contractions** are correct and which are incorrect? Put them into the table and rewrite the incorrect ones.

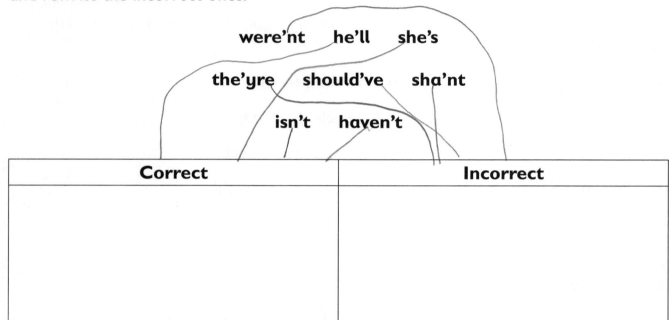

were'nt    he'll    she's

the'yre    should've    sha'nt

isn't    haven't

| Correct | Incorrect |
|---|---|
|  |  |

## Activity 2

Rewrite each sentence, changing the **contraction** into the full form.

a) We're looking forward to visiting you.  we are

b) Lily won't be able to do PE today.  would not

c) It's not our fault that the shop can't open tomorrow.  it is

# 3 Prefixes: super, anti, auto, sub, inter

Knowing the meanings of **prefixes** can help you work out the meaning of the word.

- **super** means 'above' or 'greater'.
- **anti** means 'against'.
- **auto** means 'self' or 'own'.
- **sub** means 'under'.
- **inter** means 'between' or 'among'.

## Activity 1

One word in each group has an incorrect **prefix**. Write it down and correct it.

a) international (interseptic) interview _Superterseptic_

b) antigraph      antifreeze (antisocial) _intertisocial_

c) subheading (submarket) submerge _Supermarket_

## Activity 2

Use the clues to work out the words. Write the meanings in your book. Check your answers using a dictionary.

a) auto + biography (life story) = _auto biography_

b) sub + marine (sea) = _Submarine_

c) anti + clockwise (in the same direction as the hands of a clock) =
_anti clockwise_

d) inter + national (relating to one country) = _international_

e) super + natural (relating to nature) = _Supernatural_

## Activity 3

Add the correct **prefix** to each word to make a new word.

super    sub    inter

a) _____inter_____net

b) _____Super_____market

c) _____Sub_____divide

## Activity 4

Choose the correct word from this unit to complete each sentence.

a) They ran around the park in an _____ direction.

b) Dan wanted the new sports magazine because it had an _____ with a famous footballer.

c) In her non-fiction writing, Jasmine used a heading and then three _____.

d) The _____ is great for finding out information.

e) The _____ sunk quietly into the water, ready for its mission.

f) We need to go to the _____ to buy some _____ to put on my grazed knee.

## Investigate!

Test your partner on the meanings of these **prefixes** and then see how many words you can think of for each one.

super    auto    anti    sub    inter

# 4 Prefixes: dis, mis, re, in, il, im, ir

When these **prefixes** are added to a word, the meaning is changed.

- **un**, **in** and **dis** mean 'not'.
- **mis** means 'wrong' or 'false'.
- **re** means 'again' or 'back'.

Sometimes the **prefix in** changes so that the new word it makes is easier to say.

- Before a root word starting with **l**, **in** becomes **il**.
- Before a root word starting with **m** or **p**, **in** becomes **im**.
- Before a root word starting with **r**, **in** becomes **ir**.

All of them mean 'not' or 'the opposite of'.

## Activity 1

Add the **prefix** that will turn each set of words into their opposites.

**a)** _____patient          _____polite          _____mobile

**b)** _____responsible          _____resistible          _____regular

## Activity 2

Which **prefix** do we use if something needs to be done again? Add this **prefix** to the <u>underlined</u> word in each sentence and use the new word to complete the sentence.

**a)** I'm going to <u>play</u> that song again, so I will _____.

**b)** We need to <u>decorate</u> our bedroom again, so we will _____.

**c)** The teacher has decided to <u>consider</u> the problem again, so she will _____.

**d)** Their friend had gone home but they hoped that he would <u>appear</u> again soon, he would _____.

## Activity 3

Add the correct **prefix** to each word to make a new word.

un     dis     mis

a) _____ agree

b) _____ necessary

c) _____ behave

in     il     dis

d) _____ connect

e) _____ legal

f) _____ appropriate

## Activity 4

Choose the correct word from this unit to complete each sentence.

a) The pupils were given a detention for their _____ behaviour.

b) It's fine to _____ with someone, as long as you can justify your opinion.

c) A shape with sides of different lengths is _____.

d) The chocolate cake in the shop window looked so delicious, it was _____!

e) The girl was very _____ when she didn't say 'please' or 'thank you'.

## Investigate!

Draw a table in your book and start collecting words with each of these **prefixes**, starting with the words in this unit and then from books that you read.

| un | in | dis | mis | il | im | ir | re |
|----|----|-----|-----|----|----|----|----|
|    |    |     |     |    |    |    |    |

# 5 Suffixes: ing and ed

- For most words, add **ing** or **ed**.
- When the root word ends in **e**, remove it before adding **ing** or **ed**.

  **take ⟶ taking**

- When the root word ends in a consonant, the consonant is doubled before adding **ing** or **ed**.

  **jet ⟶ jetting**

- When the root word ends in **y**, change it to **i** before adding **ed** but *not* before adding **ing**.

  **reply ⟶ replied,** but **replying**

## Activity 1

Copy the table into your book and fill in the missing words, using the rules to help you.

| Root word | ing | ed |
|---|---|---|
| jump | | |
| hike | | |
| | patting | |
| | | cried |
| | living | |

## Activity 2

Choose the correct root word to complete each sentence and then decide whether or not you need to add **ing** or **ed**.

**win        rush        fry        run        fail        smile        float**

**a)** Dad _____ some eggs for breakfast.

**b)** The frog was _____ on the lily pad.

**c)** Olly _____ happily.

**d)** Rob was _____ so fast, he was sure he would _____ the race.

**e)** She had to _____ or she'd get told off for _____ to arrive on time.

© 2016 Rising Stars UK Ltd.

# 6 Adding suffixes beginning with vowels

Look at the last syllable of the word to decide how to add the **suffix**.

- If the last syllable is stressed, the final consonant is doubled.

  **prefer** ⟶ **preferred**

- If the last syllable is not stressed, the final consonant is not doubled.

  **limit** ⟶ **limited**

- If a word ends in **e**, delete the **e** before adding the **suffix**.

  **relate** ⟶ **related**

## Activity 1

Use the rules to help you decide how to add the **suffix** to each of these words.

**a)** begin + ing = _begining_

**b)** construct + ed = _constructed_

**c)** forget + ing = _forgeting_

**d)** garden + er = _g_

**e)** commit + ed = _____

## Activity 2

Rewrite each sentence, choosing the correct spelling.

**a)** She (regretted/regreted) _____ her decision.

**b)** The church was full of people (worshiping/worshipping) _____.

**c)** He went to the bank to see the (manager/managger) _____.

**d)** The man was (sheltering/shelterring) _____ from the rain under the tree.

**e)** They loaded the cars onto the (transportter/transporter) _____, which (carried/caried) _____ them to their destination.

# 7 Suffix: ly

The **suffix ly** can be used to change **adjectives** into **adverbs**.

The exceptions are given below.

- When the root word ends in **y**, it is changed to an **i**.

  **happy** ⟶ **happily**

- When the root word ends with **le**, it is changed to **ly**.

  **gentle** ⟶ **gently**

- When the root word ends with **ic**, **ally** is added instead.

  **magic** ⟶ **magically**

## Activity 1

Change these **adjectives** into **adverbs**.

**quick** ⟶ **quickly**

**a)** safe → _____

**b)** kind → _____

**c)** real → _____

**d)** careful → _____

**e)** angry → _____

**f)** speedy → _____

## Activity 2

Change these **adverbs** into **adjectives**.

**quickly** ⟶ **quick**

**a)** loudly → _____

**b)** hungrily → _____

**c)** officially → _____

**d)** possibly → _____

## Activity 3

Complete each sentence so that it makes sense by changing the **adjective** into an **adverb**. Remember the rules!

**a)** The lion moved (cautious) _____ across the cage.

**b)** She opened her exam results (hopeful) _____.

**c)** (Final) _____, they arrived at their destination.

**d)** The clown jumped around the stage (comic) _____.

**e)** She drove her car (steady) _____.

## Activity 4

Change the **adverb** in each sentence for a different one that also makes sense. Rewrite the sentence.

**a)** Andrew rode <u>slowly</u> on his bicycle.

**b)** Lee spoke <u>joyfully</u> on the phone to her mother.

**c)** Everybody in the playground behaved <u>sensibly</u>.

**d)** It was raining <u>gently</u>.

**e)** <u>Eventually</u>, the bus driver stopped.

## Investigate!

Write some sentences of your own, using **adverbs** from this unit or ones that you have found in books you have been reading.

# 8 Suffixes: ment, ness, ful, less

All of these **suffixes** begin with a consonant, so they are added straight onto the root word.

sad ⟶ sadness

The only exception is when the root word ends in **y** and has more than one syllable – then you add **i** first.

penny ⟶ penniless

## Activity 1

One of these **suffixes** makes new words with each set of root words. Decide which one and write the new words.

**ment     ness     ful     less**

**a)** sorrow_____     hope_____     forget_____

**b)** treat_____     move_____     state_____

**c)** careless_____     wicked_____     foolish_____

## Activity 2

Add the correct **suffix** to each word to make a new word.

**ment     ness     ful     less**

**a)** loneli_____     speech_____     govern_____

**b)** tear_____     manage_____     nasti_____

**c)** aim_____     boast_____     amuse_____

**d)** disgrace_____     bossi_____     pain_____

## Activity 3

Rewrite each sentence, changing the root word by adding the **suffix** that makes most sense.

**a)** Kieran got a lot of (enjoy) _____ out of playing the piano.

**b)** Mum was impressed with the (tidy) _____ of the children's rooms.

**c)** It is (thought) _____ to drop litter.

**d)** When she lost her school jumper, she had to get a (replace) _____.

**e)** After she fell over, Jade's knee was very (pain) _____, but the first aider showed her a lot of (kind) _____.

**f)** The children were (resent) _____, as they thought the work they had been given was (end) _____ and the teachers were not showing a good example of (fair) _____.

## Activity 4

One word in each set is incorrect. Decide which one it is and then rewrite it with the correct **suffix**.

**a)** penniless        worthless      wickedless      fearless _____

**b)** government      fairment        agreement       improvement _____

**c)** treatful          beautiful        pitiful           wishful _____

**d)** cosiness         shyness         awareness       sorrowness _____

## Investigate!

Think about the **suffixes ful** and **less**. Which words can you think of that can work with both of these **suffixes** to make opposites? There are a few in this unit to start you off.

# 9 Suffix: ation

The **suffix ation** is added to **verbs** to form **nouns**.

- When the **verb** ends in a consonant, just add **ation**.

  tax ⟶ **taxation**

- When the **verb** ends in e, drop the **e** and add **ation**.

  sense ⟶ **sensation**

Exceptions include **publish** ⟶ **publication** and
**cancel** ⟶ **cancellation**.

## Activity 1

What's the rule? Decide what you need to do before adding **ation** and then write the new word.

**a)** inform → _____

**b)** tempt → _____

**c)** educate → _____

**d)** demonstrate → _____

**e)** cancel → _____

## Activity 2

Change the word in brackets from a **verb** to a **noun** so that the sentence makes sense.

**a)** They had high (expect) _____ of themselves.

**b)** At high school, the children were about to take their (examine) _____.

**c)** Romeo made a (declare) _____ of love to Juliet.

**d)** They watched an artist who was an (inspire) _____ to them.

**e)** The cook used a (combine) _____ of ingredients.

# 10 Endings: tion, ssion, sion

The suffixes **tion**, **ssion** and **sion** all make a *shun* sound. Look at the last letters of the root word to decide which one to use.

- **tion** is used if the root ends in **te** or **t**.

  **hesitate** ——→ **hesitation**

- **ssion** is used if the root word ends in **ss** or **mit**.

  **express** ——→ **expression**

  **permit** ——→ **permission**

- **sion** is used if the root word ends in **d** or **se**.

  **expand** ——→ **expansion**

  **tense** ——→ **tension**

Exceptions include **attend** ——→ **attention** and **intend** ——→ **intention**.

## Activity 1

Draw a table in your book and sort these words into the correct columns depending on their ending.

omission    inflation    promotion    extension    transmission    action

incision    percussion    temptation    conclusion    ambition    collision

| tion | ssion | sion |
|------|-------|------|
|      |       |      |

## Activity 2

**tion**, **ssion** or **sion**? Use the rules to help you to decide which **suffix** should make the *shun* sound.

**a)** televise → televishun        The ending is _____.

The correct spelling is _____.

**b)** complete → compleshun        The ending is _____.

The correct spelling is _____.

**c)** discuss → discushun        The ending is _____.

The correct spelling is _____.

## Activity 3

Change the words in brackets from **verbs** to **nouns**, choosing **tion**, **ssion** or **sion**, so that each sentence makes sense.

**a)** Hannah kept her favourite (possess) _____ in a box.

**b)** I used (divide) _____ and (subtract) _____ to answer the question.

**c)** She had to make a (confess) _____ about the stolen money.

**d)** They could hear the (explode) _____ from miles away.

**e)** There was a lot of (confuse) _____ about what had happened.

**f)** It was her (intend) _____ to put in the correct (punctuate) _____.

## Activity 4

Change the word from a **noun** to a **verb** by removing the ending. Is there anything else that you need to do?

**a)** correction → _____

**b)** creation → _____

**c)** oppression → _____

**d)** decision → _____

**e)** transmission → _____

## Investigate!

Can you use some of the words in this unit to create your own sentences?

# 11 Ending: cian

The word ending **cian** also makes a *shun* sound. It is used if the root word ends in **c** or **cs**.

magic ⟶ magician

politics ⟶ politician

## Activity 1

Which of the words below should *not* end in **cian**? Make a list and then correct them.

mathematician

televician

creacian

magician

physician

confucian

discucian

## Activity 2

**cian** is a common ending for professions. What profession do these people have? Choose the correct word to complete each sentence.

electrician   musician   technician   politician   optician

**a)** I play the violin in an orchestra. I am a _____.

**b)** I work for the government. I am a _____.

**c)** I look after people's eyes. I am an _____.

**d)** I make sure that the wires in your house are safe. I am an _____.

**e)** I work in a science laboratory. I am a _____.

# 12 Suffixes: ous, ious, eous

Some **nouns** can be changed into adjectives by adding **ous**, **ious** or **eous**. These **suffixes** mean 'full of'.

- **ous** is simply added to the root word. But, if it ends in **e**, you must delete the **e** first.

  danger ⟶ **dangerous**

  fame ⟶ **famous**

- **our** changes to **or** before **ous** is added.

  humour ⟶ **humorous**

## Activity 1

Use the meaning of the root word and the **suffix** to work out the meaning of the new adjective. One has been done for you.

humour + ous = humorous, which means 'full of humour'.

**a)** space + ious = _____, which means _____.

**b)** adventure + ous = _____, which means _____.

**c)** outrage + eous = _____, which means _____.

**d)** hilarity + ious = _____, which means _____.

## Activity 2

Copy the table into your book and fill in the missing words. One has been done for you.

| Noun | Adjective |
|------|-----------|
| *infection* | *infectious* |
| glory | |
| | mysterious |
| prosperity | |
| envy | |
| | cautious |

## Activity 3

Change the word in brackets from a **noun** to an **adjective** so that each sentence makes sense.

**a)** Stay away from the (poison) _____ snake!

**b)** The (fame) _____ singer was signing autographs.

**c)** She wore a (glamour) _____ dress to the party.

**d)** The (courage) _____ boy held on to his friend to stop him falling.

**e)** He was (fury) _____ when they wouldn't let him in.

**f)** The whole class felt (anxiety) _____ when they heard that their friend had been taken to hospital.

## Activity 4

Some **ous adjectives** do not have a root noun. Choose the correct word to complete these sentences.

**serious          previous          obvious**

**a)** She had spent the _____ week ill in bed.

**b)** The children thought that the test was easy because the answers were _____.

**c)** An ambulance arrived because this was a _____ accident.

## Investigate!

You will notice that the rules for these suffixes are quite difficult to follow. Make a note of any **ous, ious** or **eous** words that you come across and see if you can work out if they have a root word, and which rule they are following.

# 13 Root words ending in sure and ture

There are many **nouns** that have an *er* sound but are spelled **ure**. They may end with **sure** or **ture**. These endings sound similar.

- Listen carefully to hear the *t* sound in **ture**.

  **texture**

- Listen carefully to hear the *sh* sound in **sure**.

  **leisure**

## Activity 1

Choose the correct ending for each word. (Say each one aloud to check which makes sense.) Write the word.

**ture**          **sure**

**a)** pic _____

**b)** plea _____

**c)** crea _____

**d)** adven _____

**e)** enclo _____

## Activity 2

Choose a word to complete each sentence.

**measure   puncture   treasure   mixture   fracture**

**a)** The pirates found the buried _____ on the island.

**b)** To bake a cake, you need a _____ of ingredients.

**c)** Mum had to _____ Mohammed to find out how tall he was.

**d)** The X-ray showed that the bone had a _____.

**e)** The tyre had a _____ and had to be replaced.

# 14 Root words ending in tcher or cher

The word endings **tcher** and **cher** sound similar to the **ture** ending. They are mostly nouns.

**teacher, voucher**

The **suffix** to change the verb into a noun is **er**.

## Activity 1

Change these **verbs** into **nouns** by adding the **suffix er**.

**a)** stretch → _____

**b)** catch → _____

**c)** teach → _____

**d)** march → _____

**e)** watch → _____

Choose two of the new words to write in sentences.

## Activity 2

Decide which **noun** fits the definition.

pitcher    thatcher    stitcher    butcher

**a)** Someone whose job is to make roofs from dried straw is a _____.

**b)** Someone whose job is to cut up meat and sell it in a shop is a _____.

**c)** Someone whose job is to sew the finishing touches on clothes is a _____.

**d)** A baseball player who delivers the ball to the batter is a _____.

# 15 Words with the ai sound spelled ei, eigh or ey

**ei**, **eigh** and **ey** all make the same sound – *ai*, as in **pain, trail, play**.

## Activity 1

Complete the words with the correct spelling.

**a)** The horses n_____d when she approached the field.

**b)** On her birthday, Ella had _____t candles on her cake.

**c)** Part of their school uniform was a gr_____ jumper.

**d)** Th_____ sped down the snowy hill on their sl_____.

**e)** Yusra w_____ed the ingredients carefully.

**f)** The king was crowned and began his r_____n.

## Activity 2

The words below are **homophones**. Match the words to their meanings and write them in your book.

**a)**

| vain | | a tube carrying blood around the body |
| --- | --- | --- |
| vein | | thinking a lot of yourself |

**b)**

| reign | | drops of water falling from a cloud |
| --- | --- | --- |
| rain | | used to control a horse |
| rein | | the time when a king or queen is in power |

**c)**

| slay | | to kill, especially in battle |
| --- | --- | --- |
| sleigh | | a vehicle to carry people over ice and snow |

# 16 Words with the k sound spelled ch

Some English words have an unusual sound or spelling pattern because they have come from another language. Words that have a *k* sound but are spelled **ch** originally come from the Greek language.

## Activity 1

Practise making each word by putting in the **ch** and then saying it aloud.

**a)** s__eme

**b)** __aos

**c)** me__anic

**d)** s__ool

Choose two of the words and create sentences.

## Activity 2

Complete each sentence by choosing the correct word or words.

**stomach**    **anchor**    **ache**    **echo**

**chorus**    **chemist**    **character**

**a)** The ship's _____ was pulled up, ready to set sail.

**b)** A song is usually made up of a verse and a _____.

**c)** As she stood in the cave, she could hear the _____ of her own voice.

**d)** Who is your favourite _____ in the Harry Potter books?

**e)** "Ow, I think I ate too much. I've got a _____ _____!"

complained Susannah. "I must go to the _____ to get some medicine."

# 17 Words with the sh sound spelled ch

Some English words have an unusual spelling pattern because they originally came from the French language. Words that have a *sh* sound, as in **chef**, but are spelled **ch** are an example of this.

## Activity 1

Rewrite each of these words, replacing the **sh** with **ch**.

**a)** shef → _____

**b)** broshure → _____

**c)** parashute → _____

**d)** mashine → _____

**e)** moustashe → _____

Choose two of the words and create sentences.

## Activity 2

Match the words to their meanings and write them in your book. You may want to use the dictionary to help you.

| | |
|---|---|
| **chalet** | a light, transparent fabric |
| **chivalry** | small cabin or house used by holidaymakers |
| **chiffon** | a baked flan with a savoury filling |
| **quiche** | behaving in an honourable or polite way |

# 18 Words with gue and k sounds

Some English words have an unusual spelling pattern because they originally came from the French language.

- A *g* sound made with the spelling pattern **gue**, such as **catalogue**.
- A *k* sound made with the spelling pattern **que**, such as **plaque**.

## Activity 1

Decide which sound fits in each of these words – **gue** or **que**.

**a)** collea_____

**b)** techni_____

**c)** bouti_____

**d)** fati_____

Choose two of the words and create sentences.

## Activity 2

Complete each sentence by choosing the correct word or words.

> mosque    league    grotesque    tongue
>
> antique    cheque    unique

**a)** The little girl was told off for sticking out her _____.

**b)** I will write you a _____ for £50.

**c)** Manchester United have been Premier _____ champions many times.

**d)** A _____ is a place where Muslims worship.

**e)** In the attic, they found an _____ that was so _____ it

scared everyone, but it turned out to be _____ and very valuable.

# 19 Words with the s sound spelled sc

Some English words have an unusual spelling pattern because they originally come from Latin. The s sound made using the spelling pattern **sc** is an example.

**scent**, **scientific**, **conscience**

## Activity 1

Change the spelling of the *s* sound to **sc** to make each word correct.

**a)** sene → _____

**b)** cresent → _____

**c)** asent → _____

**d)** fasinate → _____

Choose two of the words and create sentences.

## Activity 2

Complete each sentence by choosing the correct word or words.

**scientist    descend    ascend    scent**

**science    scissors    scenery**

**a)** I will use the _____ to cut out this shape.

**b)** Martha was a good _____ teacher.

**c)** The _____ from the roses was beautiful.

**d)** Year 4 had to paint the background _____ for their play.

**e)** Andrew loved doing experiments and hoped to be a _____ when he grew up.

**f)** When we go up the steps, we will _____ and when we come down, we will _____.

# 20 Word families

Some groups of words are based on the same root word but have different **prefixes** or **suffixes.**

Thinking about word families can help you to spell them as they follow a pattern.

**joy, enjoyment, enjoy, enjoyed, enjoying, joyful, joyless**

- The root word is **joy** – all of the other words are made from **joy.**
- **joy** and **enjoyment** are both **nouns.**
- **enjoy, enjoyed** and **enjoying** are all **verbs.**
- **joyful** and **joyless** are **adjectives.**

## Activity 1

What is the **root word** for each of these families?

**a)** actor     action     activity     acting     _____

**b)** signal     signpost     significant     signify     _____

**c)** amended     amending     amendment     amends     _____

**d)** symbolic     symbolised     symbolism     symbols     _____

## Activity 2

Change each word from the word class it belongs to into a different word class.

**happy (adjective)** ⟶ **happily (adverb)**

**a)** build (verb) → _____ (noun)

**b)** bravely (adverb) → _____ (adjective)

**c)** cooker (noun) → _____ (verb)

**d)** pleased (verb) → _____ (noun)

**e)** belief (noun) → _____ (verb)

**f)** late (adjective) → _____ (adverb)

## Activity 3

Choose from these **prefixes** and **suffixes** to add as many words as you can to each word family. You might be able to think of some of your own as well. Use the rules you've learned to help you to add the **prefix** or **suffix**.

> dis       un       ed       ing       ful
>
> less       ment       s       er

**a)** hope _____

**b)** dance _____

**c)** thank _____

**d)** agree _____

**e)** shop _____

**f)** fair _____

**g)** cover _____

Which is the biggest word family?

## Investigate!

How many different sentences can you make using words from the same family? Choose any word family in this unit to start you off. Think carefully about the different word classes you use and how they will fit into your sentences.

31

# 21 Apostrophes for possession (singular)

When an apostrophe is used to show that something belongs to a singular noun, it goes before the **s**.

- The pen belongs to the teacher, so it is **the teacher's pen.**
- The hamster belongs to the boy, so it is **the boy's hamster.**

Singular proper nouns ending in **s** use the **'s suffix**.
**Thomas's football**

## Activity 1

Rewrite each of these, using apostrophes to show **possession**. One has been done for you.

The computer belonging to Justin is <u>Justin's computer</u>.

a) The garden belonging to Grandma is _____.

b) The book belonging to my son is _____.

c) The ticket belonging to Ali is _____.

d) The acorn belonging to the squirrel is _____.

e) The desk belonging to James is _____.

## Activity 2

Rewrite each sentence, putting the apostrophe in the correct place to show **singular possession** (each of these things has only one owner).

a) Harriet ate one of Mums cakes.

b) Milly went to her cousins house to play.

c) The dogs collar had fallen off.

d) The zoo keeper was cleaning the lions cage.

e) Cameron lost his ball so he borrowed Amirs.

# 22 Apostrophes for possession (plural)

The apostrophe is placed before the **s** to show that there is only one owner (singular).

**the girl's bag, my brother's books**

However, if there is more than one owner (plural) the apostrophe goes after the **s**.

**the bags belonging to the two girls ⟶ the two girls' bags**

**the books belonging to my brothers ⟶ my brothers' books**

**s** does not need to be added **if** the plural already ends in **s**, but the apostrophe is added *before* the **s** if the plural does not end in **s**.

**the pens belonging to the children ⟶ the children's pens**

## Activity 1

Rewrite each of these, making sure that there is an apostrophe in the correct place to show **plural possession**.

**a)** the girls clothes _____

**b)** the monkeys tails _____

**c)** the twins house _____

**d)** the cities buildings _____

**e)** the childrens games _____

## Activity 2

Complete the pairs of sentences to show **singular possession** and **plural possession**.

**The puppy sleeps in a basket, so it is the <u>puppy's basket</u>.**

**The puppies sleep in a basket, so it is the <u>puppies' basket</u>.**

**a)** The rabbit lives in a hutch, so it is _____.

The rabbits live in a hutch, so it is _____.

**b)** My son wears a shirt, so it is _____.

My three sons wear shirts, so they are _____.

**c)** The gardener grew some flowers, so they were _____.

All of the gardeners grew some flowers, so they were _____.

**d)** The mouse has whiskers, so they are _____.

The mice have whiskers, so they are _____.

## Activity 3

Change the sentences from **singular possession** to **plural possession**. Check that they make sense – there may be other words that need to be changed too.

**The robot's pencil was very sharp.**

**The robots' pencils were very sharp.**

**a)** The mug's handle fell off.

**b)** The girl's drink was quite cold.

**c)** The man's coat was in the cloakroom.

**d)** The person's dog ran through the park.

**e)** The sheep's wool was being shorn.

## Investigate!

Collect examples of words with apostrophes that you see when you are out, for example, on signs. Check that the apostrophe has been used correctly (they often aren't) and decide what it is for. Is it to show a **contraction**, the **possessive singular** or the **possessive plural**?

# 23 Homophones and near-homophones

**Homophones** are words that sound the same, or nearly the same, but are spelled differently and have different meanings.

**peace/piece, mail/male, rain/rein/reign**

Some words nearly sound the same but are spelled differently, so they are **near-homophones**.

**accept/except**

## Activity 1

The **homophones** in each pair are from different word classes. What are they?

**main is an adjective**
**mane is a noun**

**a)** meat is _____

     meet is _____

**b)** missed is _____

     mist is _____

**c)** bury is _____

     berry is _____

**d)** grate is _____

     great is _____

**e)** hear is _____

     here is _____

## Activity 2

Choose the correct **homophone** to complete each sentence.

**a)** I can't _____ what you're saying, it's too noisy. (here/hear)

**b)** There is a fun _____ on at the park today. (fare/fair)

**c)** You seem to have tied your shoelaces in a _____. (knot/not)

**d)** _____ coat is that on the floor? (Who's/Whose)

**e)** I wonder what _____ it will have if I put ice into this hot drink. (effect/affect)

## Activity 3

Read the clues and find the two **homophones** that are being described.

| mail | plane | brake | ball | mane |
|------|-------|-------|------|------|
| plain | male | main | break | bawl |

**a)** Something you fly, and something with no decoration.

_____ and _____

**b)** A man or a boy, and the post that comes through your letter box.

_____ and _____

**c)** Crying noisily, and something to throw and catch.

_____ and _____

**d)** Smash into pieces, and what you would use to stop a car.

_____ and _____

**e)** Describing something that is the most important, and the hair on the neck of a horse.

_____ and _____

## Investigate!

If you are not sure about the meanings of any of the words in this unit, look them up in the dictionary. Then practise using your new words by putting them into sentences.

# 24 Word lists

In Year 3 and Year 4 you are expected to learn to spell a list of words. Here are some ideas on how to memorise them.

- Follow spelling patterns:

  o**cc**asion, di**ff**erent and gra**mm**ar all have double consonants.

- Recognise prefixes and suffixes:

  fam**ous**, var**ious**; **dis**appear, **dis**believe

- Practise words you use regularly in other lessons:

  **opposite** and **position** (in mathematics)

- Break words down into syllables:

  **remember** ⟶ **re-mem-ber**

- Use a mnemonic, which is when you make a phrase out of letters of a word:

  **difficulty** ⟶ **Mrs D, Mrs I, Mrs FFI, Mrs C, Mrs U, Mrs LTY!**

- Use 'Look, Say, Cover, Write, Check' to learn words off by heart.

## Activity 1

Practise each set of words using 'Look, Say, Cover, Write, Check'. Focus on the spelling pattern, which is the same for all of the words.

|  | Look | Say | Cover | Write | Check |
|---|---|---|---|---|---|
| enough |  |  |  |  |  |
| though |  |  |  |  |  |
| although |  |  |  |  |  |
| thought |  |  |  |  |  |
| through |  |  |  |  |  |

|  | Look | Say | Cover | Write | Check |
|---|---|---|---|---|---|
| calendar |  |  |  |  |  |
| particular |  |  |  |  |  |
| peculiar |  |  |  |  |  |
| popular |  |  |  |  |  |
| regular |  |  |  |  |  |

| | Look | Say | Cover | Write | Check |
|---|---|---|---|---|---|
| centre | | | | | |
| century | | | | | |
| certain | | | | | |
| circle | | | | | |

## Activity 2

When you think you've learned the words, complete these sentences. The missing words are all from Activity 1 – try to work out what they are and remember how to spell them without looking.

**a)** Alice felt a little dizzy and _____ before she fell down the rabbit hole.

**b)** At our school, we believe that _____ homework helps children with their learning.

**c)** Mum said that the children had eaten _____ cake for one day.

**d)** They had to drive _____ a tunnel.

**e)** There are one hundred years in a _____.

**f)** At the disco, the children made a big _____ to dance in.

## Activity 3

Unscramble these words, which are all on the word list for Years 3 and 4. Make sure that you use all of the letters. Use the clues if you need them.

**a)** bayrlir → l_____ (you find books here)

**b)** sreawn → a_____ (goes with a question)

**c)** daugr → g_____ (looks after something important)

**d)** clybcie → b_____ (you can ride on one)

**e)** arlmteia → m_____ (wood and metal are examples)

## Investigate!

Practise clapping out the syllables to help you to learn to spell longer words. Use the word list for Years 3 and 4 and take it in turns with a partner – one person says the word and the other claps out the syllables. Then swap over for a new word.

# 25 Using a dictionary

Dictionaries can be used to:

- check the spelling of a word
- check the definition (meaning) of a word.

They are set out in alphabetical order. You need to use the first two or three letters to help you find it.

**Decide** comes before **describe**. Both begin **de**, but the third letter of **decide** is **c** which comes before the third letter of **describe** (which is **s**).

## Activity 1

Put each set of words in alphabetical order.

**a)** history     heart     group     heard

**b)** regular     reign     remember     recent

**c)** imagine     increase     island     important

**d)** special     surprise     strength     straight

**e)** exercise     experiment     enough     experience

## Activity 2

Only one spelling in each set is correct. Decide which one you think it is and then use a dictionary to check.

**a)** ilegible     illegible     illegibel     illegibal     _____

**b)** strength     strenth     strengthe     stregnth     _____

**c)** leage     leegue     league     leauge     _____

**d)** couragous     courageus     curageous     courageous     _____

**e)** ocasional     occassional     occasional     ocassional     _____

Write a sentence to explain the meaning for each of these words. If you are not sure of the meaning, look it up in a dictionary first.

**a)** natural means _____

My sentence: _____

**b)** business means _____

My sentence: _____

**c)** leisure means _____

My sentence: _____

**d)** scheme means _____

My sentence: _____

**e)** fatigue means _____

My sentence: _____

## Investigate!

How fast can you find words in the dictionary? Challenge your partner to a speed contest! Give each other a word to find and see who gets to the right page first.

# 26 Using a thesaurus

A thesaurus can be used to find alternative words to those that you already know. You can use a thesaurus to add to your vocabulary and choose words to make your writing more interesting.

## Activity 1

These are words you might find in a thesaurus. Put them in order.

**a)** How horrible? Build up to the most horrible.

unpleasant    disgusting    awful    repulsive

**b)** How nice? Build up to the nicest.

delightful    marvellous    enjoyable    splendid

**c)** How fast? Build up to the fastest.

jog    sprint    wander    gallop    hurry    amble

**d)** How strange? Build up to the strangest.

unusual    remarkable    ordinary    extraordinary    curious    everyday

## Activity 2

Choose the word that is appropriate to your sentence. Rewrite each sentence and replace **hot** with one of these words.

**sizzling    scorching    spicy    fiery**

**a)** We jumped into the pool to cool down on this hot day.

**b)** Harry has a hot temper.

**c)** That was a hot curry!

**d)** The meat was hot as they had just taken it out of the pan.

## Activity 3

Look at the picture and use a thesaurus to help you to describe it. Write down the words that you find and then put them into sentences. Think about these questions to help you.

- Where are these children?
- What are they doing?
- How are they feeling?
- What else can you see? Describe these things.

## Investigate!

Write down five **adjectives** that describe things around you. Use a thesaurus to find out if there are alternatives to those words.

# 27 Narrative (setting)

When you are writing a narrative, you need to build up a picture of what your settings are like, so that you draw the reader into your world. You can do this by thinking carefully about the words that you choose. Think about all five senses – sight, hearing, smell, touch and taste, as well as feelings. All of the time, you are adding to a word bank in your head, from ideas that you read and hear, work that you do in class and using dictionaries and thesauruses.

## Activity 1

Different words will be appropriate to use for different settings. Copy the table into your book and choose four words from the list below that you think suit each setting.

**gloomy   busy   creaking   concrete   tangled   wild   rocky**

**noisy   towering   cobbled   modern   deserted   bustling**

**silent   waves   crumbling   majestic   sparkling   misty   emerald**

**beach   vast   branches   turrets   ancient   grassy**

**colourful   tourists   dusty   dripping   chaos   doors**

| Castle | Island | City centre | Forest |
|---|---|---|---|
|  |  |  |  |

Write a sentence about each setting, using some of the words you have sorted.

a) The castle _____.

b) The island _____.

c) The city centre _____.

d) The forest _____.

## Activity 2

**Verbs** can be used to show an object doing something. Water can **shimmer**, **sparkle**, **crash**, **rumble**. Streets can **twist** and **turn**. Windows can **rattle** and stairs can **spiral**.

Rewrite each sentence, using one of these **verbs** to complete each one or choosing one of your own.

**lapped     creaked     overlooked     echoed     towered     guarded**

**a)** The waves _____ the shore.

**b)** One building _____ high above the others.

**c)** The vast cave _____ all around.

**d)** A huge wooden door _____ in the distance.

**e)** Shiny metal gates _____ the house.

**f)** The mountain village _____ the sea.

## Activity 3

Imagine a character, or characters, arriving in a setting. Choose a word from each column to make different sentences to show how the characters might behave.

| Pronouns | Verbs | Adverbs |
| --- | --- | --- |
| I | laughed | nervously |
| we | trembled | swiftly |
| he | demanded | hopelessly |
| she | skipped | excitedly |
| they | froze | forcefully |
| | crept | eagerly |
| | danced | furiously |
| | drank | suspiciously |

## Activity 4

Write your own **noun** to match each of these **adjectives**, which could relate to different settings. Then decide on the best **determiner**.

<u>a</u> hushed <u>whisper</u>
<u>some</u> creamy <u>chocolate</u>

What can you hear around you?

a) _____ blaring _____

b) _____ muffled _____

c) _____ shrieking _____

d) _____ melodic _____

What can you smell?

e) _____ smoky _____

f) _____ sweet _____

g) _____ rotten _____

h) _____ fresh _____

What can you taste?

i) _____ tangy _____

j) _____ fruity _____

k) _____ salty _____

l) _____ sour _____

## Investigate!

Now practise putting all of these ideas together to write a paragraph about a setting. Choose **nouns**, **adjectives**, **verbs** and **adverbs** to suit your setting and try to use one or two of the best words rather than throwing in lots of words that are less powerful. You want the reader to see in their heads exactly what you are describing.

# 28 Non-fiction

Non-fiction texts are set out in different ways and use different types of language, depending on their purpose. They all want to get information across to the reader clearly. These are some of the types of language and vocabulary you will find in different non-fiction texts.

- **Time conjunctions** to show chronological (time) order.

  **first, next, finally**

- **Imperative** (bossy) **verbs** to tell the reader what to do.

  **boil, jump**

- **Conjunctions** to help give more information – **causal conjunctions** to explain why.

  **because, as a result of**

- **Technical vocabulary**, relating to the topic.

  **endangered species** (in a text about animals)

- **Adverbs** to explain how or to add power to the verb.

  **carefully, extremely**

## Activity 1

Match the text type to its purpose.

**a)** To give information about a topic.

**b)** To convince people of a point of view.

**c)** To retell an important event.

**d)** To give information about how or why something happens.

**e)** To tell the reader how to do something.

persuasion

instruction

report

recount

explanation

## Activity 2

Should these text types be in chronological (time) order or not? Write 'yes' or 'no' for each one. (Hint! One of them is 'yes' and 'no', as it can be either.)

**a)** persuasion

**b)** instruction

**c)** report

**d)** recount

**e)** explanation

## Activity 3

Rewrite each sentence and <u>underline</u> the **imperative verb(s)**.

**a)** Stir the flour, milk and eggs together.

**b)** At the crossroads, turn right.

**c)** Carefully place each seed in the soil.

**d)** Draw around the shape and cut it out.

Rewrite each sentence and underline the **time conjunction**.

**e)** That evening, we arrived at our hotel.

**f)** Finally, water your seeds.

**g)** Next, fold the piece of paper in half.

**h)** We went to the cinema and then we had an ice-cream.

## Activity 4

Rewrite this persuasive text, completing it by choosing from the words below or using your own ideas.

| limited | fabulous | before | immediately |
|---|---|---|---|
| creamiest | ever | discounted | crumbliest |

This is the _____ new chocolate bar, which you have got to try

_____! It has the _____ flavour and _____ texture of

any chocolate you have _____ tasted. Selected shops are selling it at a

_____ price for a _____ time only. What are you waiting for?

Make sure you get yours _____ it sells out.

## Investigate!

Can you find different non-fiction texts in books, newspapers and magazines? Decide which text type they are, thinking about the language and vocabulary that has been used.